Gliding

poems by

Peter Solet

Finishing Line Press
Georgetown, Kentucky

Gliding

For Katherine

"And now these three remain: faith, hope and love. But the greatest of these is love."

—First Corinthians

Copyright © 2017 by Peter Solet
ISBN 978-1-63534-259-8 First Edition
All rights reserved under International and Pan-American Copyright Conventions.
No part of this book may be reproduced in any manner whatsoever without written permission from the publisher, except in the case of brief quotations embodied in critical articles and reviews.

ACKNOWLEDGMENTS

Argestes: "Candescence"
Tipton Poetry Journal: "Rosenberg Brothers, 1953," "Family Portrait, Brewster, Mass., 1981"
Asheville Poetry Review: "Two Old Friends Meet After 25 Years"
Ars Medica: "The Oncogene Waits For Darkness To Fall In The Desert"
Quiddity: "Return"

Publisher: Leah Maines

Editor: Christen Kincaid

Cover Art: Karen Roberson Powell

Author Photo: Michael Mauney © 2016

Cover Design: Elizabeth Maines McCleavy

Printed in the USA on acid-free paper.
Order online: www.finishinglinepress.com
also available on amazon.com

Author inquiries and mail orders:
Finishing Line Press
P. O. Box 1626
Georgetown, Kentucky 40324
U. S. A.

Table of Contents

Candescence 1
Air Raid Drill, 1952 2
…nearly midnight 3
The Summer of Fifty-Four 4
Rosenberg Brothers, 1953 5
Two Old Friends Meet After 25 Years 6
First Snow 7
Passage 8
Gliding 9
The night I heard 10
Color Line, 1957 11
The Oncogene Waits for Darkness to Fall in the Desert 12
Winter Solstice 13
Epistle 14
Family Portrait, Brewster, Mass, 1980 15
The Walk 16
In An Ancient Wood 18
Return 19
Rachel's Bridge 21
Soliloquy (Kid in Home for Children) 22
I call you out 25
Children's Lament 26
Burial 27
This Ain't No Caddy 28

Candescence

In the dust-gray
clatter of the D train,
below Brooklyn's quilted streets,
I watched a boy put
his hand on the curve of his girlfriend's hip
as they stood face to face
in yellow spotted light.

It was far gone into night,
drunks passed out lengthwise
on the seats, a dun-dressed man
dozing behind the *Daily News,*
the couple returning rumpled
from regions beyond,
and me at thirteen, in shadow.

I watched them from across
the aisle, so conscious of my gathering
erection, needing so little–a glimpse
of bra as her bare arm reached
for the overhead strap. His hand
on her hip spoke to me of possession,
and I knew from some ancient place
she had acquiesced and would acquiesce
more in an embrace I could
only imagine, had imagined, many times.

These decades later, the mystery
of that embrace is long gone
and my body has found its place.
I see them, sheen-skinned, radiant
against the black train window;
I am frozen in desire; not to possess the girl
but to be possessed by the light.

Air Raid Drill, 1952

First, Miss Epstein shows the film
in my darkened
second-grade classroom—

a speck, a ball, a moon, a sun,
a flash, over in a flash—

Then the heart-stab siren's call to prayer,
the dive beneath my desk,
head tucked under bloodless hands,
ID tag cool against my neck.

And I'm sure I hear
the warden's cries, the sound
of bees. the windows
crack, the suck-air wind—

...nearly midnight,

and the girl, bloodied and spent,
clings to a dream
of tall trees and cold streams,
of a breeze across
her loose black hair.
And then her newborn
blindly flails, wails her
awake in starlight.

She can't imagine holding
his pierced, broken body,
this infant at her breast,
breathing her as she breathes him.
Later her yes will be remembered,
but now, at this hour...

The Summer of Fifty-Four

All day I rode the waves, or trapped fiddler crabs in a jar, or played
SkeeBall on the boardwalk, closed out my first decade
turning red and blue, salty and prune-skinned.

My grandma took a beach bungalow, plucked me
from baked Manhattan to breezy Far Rockaway, a province
past the subway, outside the known world. Grandma
was wise, knew which bus to take and when to turn mean.
One boy-crazy sister was more guest than family,
and so my little brother, cousin, parakeet and cat
filled the space with me, forced the place to earn its keep.

I took little note of wars and tribulations, my father's joblessness,
my mother's latest pregnancy, another sister's delinquencies.
Away from parents, school, neighborhood thugs,
each day unfurled clean, like a waterfall.
Love was a wave crashing over my head,
driving me to the sand with such force
I would get lost. I lived one last time unknowing of girls
and all they possessed, all I would want. My religion
was an ice-cream cone cajoled from weighty hands,
how Willie did that day.

At summer's end Carol appeared, flooded streets from sea to bay.
I would have gone away on her back had she asked,
but she sailed off, and the water receded,
leaving detritus and displaced, choking sand.

Rosenberg Brothers, 1953

In this hard-grained photo
from the Daily News,
you don't know
that you walk for the final time
across the iron-curtained courtyard
of Sing Sing, where
your parents wait.

You are six and ten.
Your wear dungarees and polo shirts.
A heavy-bodied lawyer is holding
your hands, as if you were
skipping in the park.
Dodgers is emblazoned on your caps.
You are smiling.

Two Old Friends Meet after 25 Years

We sniffed,
old dogs greeting
each other after
so many years.
You've been around
I see,
Like me.
You smelled of anticipation
and musty sores
topped with a maraschino cherry of wit.
You smelled the same,
only better.

First Snow

Snow will be here by week's end
to finish off the flower bed
and age the stubborn oak again.
I've unearthed the fat gray comforter
that feathered our winter bed
when you, me and the thick-furred cat
holed up like old ladies waiting
for the melt to come someday.

One year the storm surprised us,
gripped you, a summer stalk,
broke you in a blaze of infernal ice.
Every year it settles through the milk sky,
burning in the space it grew.

The cat and I have given up hunting.

Passage

You roam the hills,
all sinew and laser sharpness,
looking, forgetting
how the ground smells,
the curl of air in your face,
the cool breath of spring
heaving everywhere.

The shadow of thought
spreads like honey
over your eyes, gathers
in pools on your tongue.
Yet look you must,
 'till grace lets you rest, another heart
breaks, another nail is driven home.

Gliding

The summer my father really began to die,
he feverishly wandered into the wrong house,
argued vehemently with the middle-aged couple
who lived there hawking antiques to hurried summer people.
He shook a white-tufted fist and cursed at their audacity;
they called the police.

In the hospital he was given antibiotics by vein.
Antibiotics, antipsychotics: the fever
was a cold moon on his horizon.

I found out about his other illnesses: bleeding ulcers,
urinary tract infections, clogged carotid arteries
that starved his brain.

Near the end he called himself
the new village character,
the guy who checks
to see whether you have the proper sticker
to park at the beach.
I always seemed to have last year's,
or this year's had been stolen.

Afterward I think how juicy
while I glide over the lawn,
combing for sleek nightcrawlers.
I am hot with excitement, trapping them
in the wet grass where they lounge full length,
barely touching the home hole. My index finger
swoops from above to cut off that route,
like my father's swooping Stuka fists.

The night I heard

the bark of wardens,
siren shrieks, the drone of engines;
saw hurried terror
on the sidewalk below,
and a sky studded black with bombers;
I fled to where my parents slept,
but they were oblivious of this war,
of a life being spent in absentia.

When my father awoke
he heard the rat-a-tat-tat
of my heart, saw my thin white arms
grasp for cover, and he punched me,
a mighty punch that emptied me,
sent me deeper into hiding,
closer to knives and loaded rifles,
inhabited by savage dreams.

Color Line, 1957

Once, in the doldrums of summer,
a black kid bopped down my block.
He snatched the pink Spaldeen I'd bought,
with a flick I caught too late.

He fled across the color line,
toward safety, his turf, his block,
sure no white kid would follow,
do what he had done.

But I chased him,
grabbed the neck of his shirt,
and we pulled each other down;
I rolled with his punches
and he with mine, 'till an Irish cop
scruffed me, took me back,
the ball jammed in my pocket.

The Oncogene Waits for Darkness to Fall in the Desert

Wild,
the oncogene—p53—can be found
on the short arm of chromosome 17,
a patch of shadow perched
in saguaro's thorny nook.
Under Sonoran sun
nothing moves,
but in moonlight
missense and nonsense cavort
and wing-tip their way through
oncogene's 11 exons,
trying all her locks.
When the dance is over,
p53, no longer wild,
leaves a legacy
of immortality.

Winter Solstice

Brittle, brown meadow grass
huddles secrets and melancholy songs,
lies flat, impervious to the nervous wind
that must go 'round and 'round.
And though I stoke the fire high
the house stays cold, immune;
road ice enters, makes a home;
even the cat gives up,
takes communion alone.

Growls of monkish chants descend,
flicker through my roof,
incense swaying to and fro,
licking in my throat,
words free-basing in my brain,
solace and solitaire shimmering.
My foot tramping loud,
the ground frozen, at last.

Epistle

Hey man, maybe you're just a showy show-off,
raising the dead, casting out devils,
turning water into wine,
but you ain't practical, if you know what I mean—
I mean raising the dead
might be mighty upsetting
to folks who was rejoicing,
or maybe wouldn't have cared.
Those devils? Where the hell did they
disappear to? Find another home?
As for the water into wine trick
you pulled at that wedding,
who do you think cleaned up the vomit and pee?

And why do we need to see your tricks anyway?
You either the Son of God or you ain't,
and if you are, ain't that enough?

Family Portrait, Brewster, Mass, 1980

In that moment the camera
seizes Cape Cod pines
in their sandy, shallow beds—
roots frantic for purchase,
forever mining for water—
straighten and rise, as though
a crooked world could be righted,
a frame for us
who could only face the camera
and hope.

The Walk

After the turkey, the asparagus and pea casserole,
After the sweet potatoes and hot rolls,
After we lolled like fish-choked penguins,
Claiming we would never eat again,
The blessing and giving of thanks already forgotten,
We took a walk, to digest, shrink calories,
Our stomachs spilling
Over waistbands into territory we'd
Sworn we'd never set foot in.

The old folks reclined in thick chairs,
Shooing us into the chilled air.
Naw, they said, we don't want to go,
Too tired, too full, too drowsy in the warm-house blanket,
The golden comfort of TV football droning through the house.

We are outdoors then, glad for the musk of moldering leaves,
The breeze that threatens to bring rain
Before day's end. We move along the idle street,
An amorphous braided rug, some in the center, some on the fringes.

The boys and young men toss a Nerf ball in godly spirals,
Sure of their timeless bodies, then watch in secret horror
The older men test muscles that have stiffened
And faded over yet another year, used for no more
Than driving the rare nail, twisting the occasional lid.
The girls and women walk with the easy roll of satisfaction,
Their loud laughter spicing the air, the girls eager,
The women joyous in the moments the ball comes their way
like the toy it is, free of challenge, the little kids winding among us.

Then we are back, the ball put away for another year,
The children buzzing, hatching new plots by the minute
While their parents drift off like a languorous herd.
We have walked enough, someone says, to speak of dessert,
As if an afterthought, a conspiracy of silent contemplation.
Out come the pies—apple and chess, and the cakes—caramel
And yellow, and belts are let out another notch in surrender.
We try all, just smidgens we declare, before going back for seconds,
Even thirds, our sweet wickedness swept away in waves of pleasure.
Praise is heaped upon the proud bakers, the cooks,
the hosts, who nod with outward humility and inner pride.

The coffee arrives in fine china cups, the beginning of the end.
Yes, we say, we could use another walk now, but dusk
Has fallen, the promised rain has begun, headaches are budding,
And the children have nodded off in corners. In muted light
We assemble them, the littlest draped over bedded shoulders.
Gather jackets and hats—the sound of zippers proclaiming day's end—
And piles of leftovers that will serve us with fond thoughts
And hidden resentments for days.

We hug and kiss and spill into cars, and the hosts watch
Our tail lights smooth into the darkness. All is put to rest,
In hibernation, on ice till next year. And don't we wonder, in private,
Trembling, how the rug will look then?

In an Ancient Wood

In an ancient wood,
in a field of fern and lily,
I came across a long-dead hickory
lying exposed, torn head pillowed
against a mottled boulder,
gray-white striations where bark
once kept out sun and snow,
moss bearded with creamsicle-colored fungi,
outrageous frolic on a green blanket.

Return

Each time you appear
You are stronger.
You sit in my kitchen
Next to the knives,
In my car around
The steering wheel,
Near any rifle
That happens to be nearby.

You would like me
To welcome you
But then you beat upon
The steel-stitched seam
Of my aging chest.
You would breathe of my breath,
Flow in my blood,
Contract with my heart.
You would see with my eyes
And root out memories
Of silence and shipwreck
Till you either triumph
Or I take you in.

This is your burden,
The misfortune of your being.

Yet you are my darling,
The grandest part of me,
The garden path,
The bright disk of hope.

A child is not dust
To be pushed across
The room, not a trussed
Up cushion for

Cursed lives.
A child does not lack
For a god,
In spite of affliction.

Rachel's Bridge

        Bridge meds they're called,
            what they gave her when she ran out,
as if she was strung out on crack or smack
           instead of hearing voices
                              taking   off

       so after she got them she went back
           to where she came from
until her bridge ran out again and she had
to hold a knife to her throat to get into St. Joe's,
         what you do these days.

            Three days she floated on dying,
      paper shoes, locked in, cold room.   .

      They spoke of sending her to Broughton,
locked up for months, comatose. No   way,
      been   there,
            done   that.

                            She held tight, got
     away with her kids,
till they took them
        again,
           and she was off her meds,
               away
                       under the bridge,
          out of sight,
                  out of her mind.

     There was no   holding her.

         She turned 29 in June.
         In October she swallowed the bridge.

Soliloquy (Kid in Home for Children)

there's three of us here
JJ Pit Bull and me
boys in the house
the girls have
their own space
so what
they're real dogs

this place is ok
i go along

two house parents
whatta joke
real clean
jesus this/jesus that
load of crap

this place is ok
i go along

social workers
sit around
ask me about goals
stuff i need to work on
i play
with their heads
just don't ask me
about the knife again

this place is ok
i go along

the girls in school
they know
where i live
so what
i'm smart
gonna be a pilot
what goes on in my pants
is my own business

this place is ok
i go along

saw my mom
in court last time
looking good
clean
in a program
said she loves me
wants me back
not the first time
but she's the only one
that does love me
she's my mom

this place is ok
i go along

judge frowned
you just got out of jail
no job no place to live
can't stop using
turning tricks
it's your choice
your drugs or
your child

this place is ok
i go along

a week later
no one could find her

someday there's gonna be some blood around here
some serious blood.

I call you out

o robed and mitred men,
you who vowed the wrong vow
and damned women raped by any male
in Kenya, South Africa, Zimbabwe,
left children to starve, and worse.

Don't tell me the seed
must not be stilled
but planted in uterine dirt
that waits inert and thus
is unworthy of protection,
protection you save
for cassocks and albs.

Children's Lament

She bore us then forgot us
left us swift and left us sure

Left us for pleasure
but she was young
and pleasure always
screams for more.

Left us for work for a bed
for a promise of freedom
for Jesus for dead.

She left us in the morning
by the side of the road,
in the cool, cool evening
while we dreamt;
sometimes she left us
in rivers of red.

And we who are left
weep at each leaving
and when the leaving is done
we weep for the bearing

weep for the love of the bearing.

Burial

Up on the hill, past the old barn
where we did your secret stuff,
past the hollow where a house
used to stand, a house
as real as real could be,
but gone now, history
that shifts like a pale mirage.

Up on that naked spot,
in a mire of thorns,
out near the very top of that ancient hill,
I tried to bury you, but you were still
alive, very much alive, and even
a thousand knives couldn't do you in
any more than wakefulness can kill a dream.

I've seen you perform
the trick of death many times,
and I have gone for the shovel,
prepared the rooms for a wake,
counted down the seconds
only to awaken on my knees,
fear leaking in a smelly pool
at the foot of my bed.

But in the end, I confess, burial is not the issue,
not if death is a requirement.

So roll me in the blue-black leaves of winter,
shoot me through with ice,
tear my fingers from their sockets,
leave me to my sketchy world,
and I will leave you to do your own burying,
in your own time, by yourself.

This ain't no Caddy

       This ain't no Cadillac, friend,
no long-nosed limo poised in space,
nothing you might settle for.

       A Cadillac bleeds chrome, leaves a scent
a man can follow, follows a man
into every room of the house,
runs the roads like your long-ago youth,
scoffing at limits and lesser gods.
She rides you past despair, outdistances
your imagination, your bloody aches,
your two-bit pains.

       Go on and slide your sorry butt across her leather,
touch her dash, kneel into her, lean on her,
prepare to yield to her perfumed fire and her high-toned pistons,
the sweet song of her Chesterfield voice.
Let her take you in soft, slow murmurs that slither
up your pitiful back, caress your ear
with the winds of her old-time religion,
her promise of heaven on earth,
your baptism in her honeyed river.

       Prostrate yourself in the frigid darkness,
pray and pray, roll in the dirt and speak in tongues,
it'll do no good, 'cause this ain't no Cadillac,
brother.

Pete **Solet** was born in Maryland and grew up in Manhattan in the Fifties and Sixties. His writing endeavors began in earnest, some thirty years later, as an undergraduate at North Carolina State University, studying with Professor Gerald Barrax.

Since that time, he has been privileged to participate in numerous workshops and classes, mostly through the Glen Workshop in Santa Fe and also in the Great Smokies Writing Program at the University of North Carolina, Asheville. Many poets have influenced him, notably Langston Hughes, Seamus Heaney, Richard Hoffman, and Linda McCarriston.

He retired in 2008 after careers in journalism, auto repair, and clinical research, among others, and has lived with his wife Katherine in the mountains of Western North Carolina since 1999. His three children and two grandchildren live in Maine and Massachusetts. He is a former Guardian ad Litem and currently serves in the Society of St. Vincent de Paul.

www.ingramcontent.com/pod-product-compliance
Lightning Source LLC
LaVergne TN
LVHW041506070426
835507LV00012B/1373